IF HOTDOGS COULD TALK

What Stupid Things Would They Say?

WINSTON REDFORD

planksip®

For information contact; **planksip.org**.

Book and Cover design by planksip® publishing.

ISBN:

ONE

The Ketchup Conspiracy

A FIRST-PERSON NARRATIVE BY A PARANOID HOTDOG

"They say ketchup doesn't belong on hotdogs. But who decided that? The mustard cartel?"

Listen, I'm not saying **they** are out to get us.

I'M JUST SAYING it's a little suspicious that every time I try to tell someone the truth, they take a bite out of me.

COINCIDENCE? I don't think so.

LET me start at the beginning.

I WAS A NORMAL HOTDOG ONCE. Just another wiener in the pack, waiting for my time on the grill. I didn't ask for this life. I didn't choose to be awake, to be self-aware. But something changed. One day, as I lay in the fridge next to a carton of eggs (who, by the way, are way too comfortable with their mortality), I overheard something that shook me to my very bun.

SOME GUY at the barbecue said, **"You know, real hotdogs don't use ketchup."**

I FROZE. What did he mean, *real* hotdogs? Was I… fake? Was this some kind of existential crisis, or was something deeper at play? Was ketchup—sweet, innocent ketchup—being *silenced*?

THAT WAS the moment I started asking questions. And buddy, let me tell you—once you start asking questions, things get weird.

HOW A CONSPIRACY THEORY **Starts**

CONSPIRACY THEORIES ARE a lot like gas station sushi—most people should know better, but somehow, someone always falls for them.

. . .

AND THE TRUTH IS, humans **love** conspiracies. Your brains are wired to look for patterns, and when there isn't one, you just **make one up**. Your ancestors did it all the time. They saw weird lights in the sky and thought, *Yep, aliens*. They saw a weird shadow in the woods and thought, *Better start a religion about this*. That's how you ended up with things like the Loch Ness Monster, Bigfoot, and multi-level marketing schemes.

IT'S NO DIFFERENT TODAY.

ONE GUY on the internet says, **"I don't trust the government."**

A SECOND GUY REPLIES, **"I also don't trust the government."**

A THIRD GUY JOINS IN, **"Maybe the government is actually made of lizard people."**

BOOM. Now there's a subreddit with 200,000 followers and a guy selling t-shirts that say, **"WAKE UP, SHEEPLE."**

. . .

THAT'S how easy it is.

AND NOW, I was about to fall down the same rabbit hole.

THE KETCHUP COVER-UP

THE DEEPER I LOOKED, the weirder things got.

KETCHUP USED to be **everywhere** on hotdogs. I saw the photos, the historical evidence. But then, suddenly, people started saying ketchup was *wrong*. That it was *childish*. That a *real* hotdog only had mustard, onions, and maybe some suspiciously neon-green relish.

WHO DECIDED THIS?

WHO MADE THE RULES?

AND MORE IMPORTANTLY–**WHAT were they hiding?**

I STARTED LOOKING into the big names. The National Mustard Association? More powerful than you'd think.

The Hotdog Council? **Suspiciously well-funded.** I even found an old newspaper clipping from 1972 with the headline:

"KETCHUP DECLARED UNFIT FOR HOTDOGS—WHO **Benefits?"**

THE WHO? The World Health Organization? What did they have to do with this?

THE DEEPER I LOOKED, the crazier it got.

THAT'S the thing about conspiracy theories. They start small. Harmless. Just a question. But then you start connecting dots that maybe *shouldn't* be connected. You start seeing patterns where there are none. And suddenly, you're alone in a dark room, surrounded by crumpled-up papers, whispering, *"It all makes sense now."*

THE CLASSIC CONSPIRACY **Playbook**

ONCE YOU START STUDYING conspiracy theories, you realize they all follow the same basic recipe.

.   .   .

STEP 1: **Take Something Confusing**

HUMANS DON'T LIKE UNCERTAINTY. If something weird happens, people want an explanation. The simpler, the better.

FOR EXAMPLE:
- *Why do people sometimes see weird lights in the sky?*
- Reasonable answer: Airplanes, satellites, or meteors.
- Conspiracy answer: Aliens are abducting cows for secret milk experiments.
- *Why did my WiFi go down?*
- Reasonable answer: Your router sucks.
- Conspiracy answer: The government is testing mind-control waves.

AND IN MY CASE:
- *Why do people say ketchup doesn't belong on hotdogs?*
- Reasonable answer: Some people just prefer mustard.
- Conspiracy answer: **BIG MUSTARD IS SILENCING THE TRUTH.**

STEP 2: **Add a Villain**

. . .

A GOOD CONSPIRACY needs a **bad guy**. Someone powerful. Someone shadowy. Someone with **way too much influence over hotdog condiments.**

I HAD A LOT OF SUSPECTS:
- The **National Mustard Association**
- The **Chicago Hotdog Cartel**
- The **FDA** (which, for some reason, is obsessed with defining what a sandwich is?)

BUT THE BIGGEST SUSPECT?

BIG RELISH.

THAT'S RIGHT. Relish has been waiting for its moment. It knows it's the least popular condiment, but what if it could destroy ketchup **and** take its place?

THINK ABOUT IT.

STEP 3: **Make It Impossible to Disprove**

THE BEST CONSPIRACIES are **just vague enough** that you can never fully debunk them.

. . .

IF SOMEONE SAYS, *"The moon landing was fake,"* and you show them HD footage, they'll say, *"Ah, but that's just what they want you to believe."*

IF SOMEONE SAYS, *"Birds aren't real,"* and you show them a real bird, they'll say, *"That's a government surveillance drone in disguise."*

AND NOW, whenever I try to talk about the Ketchup Conspiracy, people just roll their eyes and say, *"Oh, you're one of those hotdogs."*

CLASSIC GASLIGHTING.

THE DUMBEST THINGS **People Say About Conspiracies**

ONCE YOU START LOOKING into conspiracies, you realize people say **some truly stupid things.**

1. **"If it were true, we'd know about it."**

. . .

OH, really? You ever heard of **Area 51**? **Watergate**? The fact that your local fast-food place *definitely* has a secret menu but won't tell you?

SECRETS EXIST, people.

2. **"They couldn't keep it hidden for this long."**

HAVE YOU MET HUMANS? People keep secrets **all the time.** Your grandma has secrets. Your **dog** has secrets. If your best friend can hide the fact that they still watch reality TV, the government can definitely cover up the truth about condiments.

3. **"My cousin's neighbor's uncle totally worked for the CIA and told me…"**

AH YES, the most reliable source of information: **your cousin's neighbor's uncle.**

SO… **Is the Ketchup Conspiracy Real?**

I DON'T KNOW. Maybe. Maybe not.

. . .

WHAT I **DO** KNOW IS that the mustard industry **has a lot of money** and **a lot of power**. I also know that whenever I bring this up, I mysteriously end up on someone's plate.

COINCIDENCE?

I'LL LET YOU DECIDE.

BUT IF I disappear after this, remember: **I WAS RIGHT.**

TWO

The Existential Bun Crisis

A FIRST-PERSON NARRATIVE BY A PHILOSOPHICALLY
OVERWHELMED HOTDOG

"Am I a sandwich? A taco? Or something... more?"

I was fine until someone called me a sandwich.

IT WAS SUPPOSED to be a normal day. Sun shining. Barbecue sizzling. The usual existential dread hanging in the air like overcooked bratwurst. But then, out of nowhere, I heard it.

"TECHNICALLY, A HOTDOG IS A SANDWICH."

I FROZE. The bun around me clenched slightly. A sandwich? Was that what I was? I mean, sure, I fit *some* of the criteria—bread, filling, edible—but did that *define* me?

· · ·

AND IF NOT A SANDWICH... then what?

MY ENTIRE WORLD crumbled faster than a cheap grocery store bun.

THUS BEGAN MY EXISTENTIAL CRISIS.

THE ABSURDITY **of Identity (And Also, Jean-Paul Sartre Was a Weirdo)**

THE PROBLEM with being self-aware is that once you start asking *what* you are, there is **no good answer.** Just ask any existentialist. They spent their entire careers sitting in dark cafés, chain-smoking and muttering things like,

"LIFE HAS NO INHERENT MEANING." – Sartre
   "Existence precedes essence." – Also Sartre
   "I am my own negation." – Some guy who definitely needed a nap

NOT EXACTLY AN UPLIFTING BUNCH. But I get it. I, too, was questioning my purpose.

· · ·

I TURNED to philosophy for guidance, but that only made things worse. Take **Albert Camus**, for example. He argued that life is meaningless, and the only rational response is to embrace *the absurd*. You know what's absurd? A hotdog reading Camus. That's where I was at.

AND THEN, of course, there's **Friedrich Nietzsche,** who basically looked at the universe and went, *"God is dead, and so are your comforting illusions."*

WELL, Nietzsche, thanks for nothing. I was looking for answers, not a philosophical slap in the face.

WHAT EVEN IS A HOTDOG?

LET'S break it down logically. If we're using rigid categories, I should fit neatly into one.

OPTION 1: **I'm a Sandwich**
- Bread? Check.
- Filling? Check.
- Exists in the food section of a gas station? Check.

BUT HERE'S THE PROBLEM–IF I'm a sandwich, then so is a taco. And if a taco is a sandwich, then so is a burrito. And if a burrito is a sandwich, **society collapses under the weight of its own absurdity.**

OPTION 2: **I'm a Taco**
- One continuous piece of folded bread? Check.
- Portable? Check.
- Usually sold at stadiums by a guy who calls everyone "boss"? Also check.

BUT IF I accept that I'm a taco, then what does that make a **pita?** A pita is also folded bread. But a pita is never called a taco. So where do we draw the line?

OPTION 3: **I Transcend Labels**

THIS IS where existentialism really kicks in. Maybe I **am** a sandwich **and** a taco **and** something else entirely. Maybe I exist in a **fluid state of identity,** refusing to be boxed in by rigid definitions.

AND THAT'S when I realized…

I WAS **HAVING A BUN CRISIS.**

. . .

THE BUN PROBLEM: **More Than Just a Carb Issue**

I LOOKED DOWN at my bun, my loyal casing, my warm embrace.

AND SUDDENLY, I wasn't sure if it was really *me*.

FOR MY ENTIRE LIFE, I had taken my bun for granted. But what if my bun was just... *something I had*? Not something I *was*?

AFTER ALL, if someone **takes me out of the bun, am I still a hotdog?**

IF THEY PUT me in a lettuce wrap instead, am I still *me*?

OR AM I something else entirely?

THIS IS where the parallels to gender identity kick in. Because if a bun is just something that holds me—but not something that defines me—then who am I to say what kind of bun is *correct*?

· · ·

I COULD BE A **BUNLESS** HOTDOG. A **gluten-free** hotdog. A **croissant-wrapped** hotdog. And none of these versions would make me *less* of a hotdog.

THIS REALIZATION SHATTERED my mind like a ketchup packet under a steel-toed boot.

BECAUSE IF *I* can't define what a hotdog truly is... then maybe humans shouldn't be so quick to define each other.

THE DUMB THINGS **Philosophers Say (That Weirdly Apply to My Crisis)**

1. **"Man is condemned to be free." – Sartre**

AH YES, the classic **Sartrean nightmare.** The idea that we have no predetermined essence and must define ourselves. You know what's scary? Having to figure out who you are **while being cooked over an open flame.**

2. **"If God did not exist, it would be necessary to invent Him." – Voltaire**

. . .

THIS ONE MADE ME THINK: *If hotdogs didn't exist, would humans have invented them anyway?* The answer is **yes**, because you people will put anything in a bun and charge $7.99 for it.

3. **"He who has a why to live can bear almost any how." – Nietzsche**

COOL, Friedrich. But what if my "why" is **being devoured by someone who doesn't even chew properly?**

HOW TO SURVIVE **an Existential Crisis (If You're a Hotdog)**

AT THIS POINT, I was spiraling. I needed **answers.** I needed **guidance.** I needed **someone to tell me what I was.**

I CONSIDERED GOING TO THERAPY, but most therapists refuse to see talking food items (rude). So instead, I turned to **The Three Great Solutions to Existential Dread:**

1. **Denial:** Pretend the crisis doesn't exist. ("Hotdogs have no identity issues. Everything is fine.")

2. **Distraction:** Focus on something else. ("Maybe I should start a food blog.")

3. **Acceptance:** Embrace the chaos. ("I am neither sandwich nor taco. I am **hotdog.**")

THAT THIRD ONE sounded the most *zen*, so I decided to go with it.

FINAL THOUGHTS **from a Deeply Confused Hotdog**

IN THE END, I realized something important.

I DON'T NEED **a label to exist.**

I DON'T HAVE to be a sandwich. Or a taco. Or anything else.

I CAN JUST BE **ME**–A delicious, slightly overcooked, endlessly questioned **hotdog.**

AND MAYBE, just maybe, that's enough.

. . .

NOW, if you'll excuse me, I have to go sit under a heat lamp and rethink my entire existence.

THREE

The Hotdog Marathoner

A FIRST-PERSON NARRATIVE BY A WIENERMOBILE-WORTHY ATHLETE

"If I run fast enough, will I turn back into a sausage?"

I was **not** built for running.

I WAS BUILT for **being admired at cookouts, reclining in a warm bun**, and perhaps, if destiny allowed, taking a leisurely spin on a rotisserie roller. I was **not** meant to be laced into a pair of tiny neon shoes and dragged through the streets at an ungodly hour.

AND YET, here I am—**training for a marathon.**

WHY? Because apparently, **everything is a marathon now.**

. . .

HOW EVERYTHING BECAME **a Marathon**

ONCE UPON A TIME, running was **a last resort**.

YOU RAN when you were **chased**—by a bear, by the cops, or by an angry street vendor after you asked if the hotdogs were "ethically sourced." Running was not something you **chose** to do.

THEN, somewhere along the way, a special kind of human **ruined it for the rest of us.**

I CALL them **The Running People.**

THESE ARE NOT normal humans who sometimes jog to get fresh air. No. These are **the people who wake up at 4 AM, throw on $300 shoes, and "just get a quick 12 miles in" before breakfast.**
- **Marriage?** *"It's a marathon, not a sprint."*
- **Starting a business?** *"Gotta train for the long haul."*
- **Raising a child?** *"You just have to pace yourself."*
- **Trying to leave a conversation with them?** *"Not until I tell you about my personal best mile time."*

. . .

RUNNING People see the world as **one giant endurance event.** Everything requires **training, pacing, and pushing through the pain.**

PAIN IS, in fact, a **huge** part of their personality.

"IF YOU HAVEN'T LOST a **toenail, are you even a runner?"**

EXCUSE ME? If I lose a toenail, I'm going to **the hospital, not a motivational Facebook group.**

THE STUPID THINGS **Runners Say**

ONCE I GOT DRAGGED into this world, I realized that runners don't just **act** differently—they **speak a different language.** And it's **insane.**

1. **"You don't run to get in shape—you get in shape to run."**

THIS IS **PEAK CULT TALK.**

. . .

SO RUNNING **DOESN'T** MAKE you fit? You have to be fit **before** you run? So why run at all? What is the **end goal?** Is this a **pyramid scheme for sneakers?**

2. "THE FIRST MILE IS A LIAR."

FIRST OF ALL, **miles don't talk.**

SECOND, what is this, some kind of **philosophical gaslighting?** What's the **second mile's** deal? Is it a compulsive truth-teller?

SPOILER ALERT: **all the miles were liars.**

3. **"Pain is just weakness leaving the body."**

NO. Pain is my **body begging me to stop.**

PAIN IS **A WARNING SIGN**, like when someone orders sushi at a gas station. You don't **push through** it—you **reevaluate your life choices.**

4. **"I just got my PR down to 6:30."**

.   .   .

OH WOW, **6 minutes and 30 seconds?** Cool. I got mine down to **never.**

5. **"Runner's high is better than any drug."**

THIS IS FALSE. I have **seen drugs.** Drugs **do not require a $180 hydration vest** and **four months of training.**

THE TRANSFORMATION **into a Running Addict**

AT FIRST, I hated running. Every step felt like **someone was hitting me with a meat tenderizer.** My legs burned, my lungs felt like **two expired balloons**, and I was sweating in places I didn't even know could produce sweat.

BUT THEN... something happened.

AT SOME POINT, **I stopped fighting it.** I stopped questioning **why** I was doing it. I stopped wondering **if** I was built for this.

.   .   .

I BECAME ONE OF THEM.

IT STARTED SMALL.

I CAUGHT myself **nodding knowingly** when someone mentioned their "cadence."

THEN, I found myself **Googling foam rollers.**

ONE DAY, I even said the cursed words:

"I CAN'T. **I have a long run tomorrow."**

THAT WAS the moment I knew **it was over for me.**

THE TRAGIC PHYSICAL **Toll of Running**

LET'S talk about **what happens to the body of a hardcore runner.**

- **Toenails?** *Gone. Yeeted into the void.*
- **Knees?** *A distant memory.*
- **Body fat?** *It left in the late 90s and never came back.*
- **Caloric intake?** *12,000 a day, mostly in gel form.*

- **Social life?** *Nonexistent.*

THERE IS no **human being** on Earth skinnier than **a dedicated marathoner.** These people have **negative body fat.** They are **built entirely out of stubbornness and electrolyte packets.**

AND YET, despite looking like **animated skeletons with headbands,** they will **brag about their carb-loading routine** like they're training for the Olympics.

"OH, **I eat SO much. You wouldn't believe it. I had THREE almonds yesterday."**

CONGRATULATIONS, Steve. That's almost **half a calorie.**

THE "THIS IS NORMAL" **Lie**

YOU EVER NOTICE how runners **pretend that none of this is weird?**

THEY WILL **CASUALLY** mention that they ran **14 miles before work,** and then be like,

. . .

"ANYWAY, HOW'S YOUR MORNING BEEN?"

HOW HAS MY MORNING BEEN?

I WOKE UP, drank **an entire pot of coffee**, and considered taking **a nap.** Meanwhile, you've **conquered the Oregon Trail before sunrise.**

OR MY PERSONAL FAVORITE:

"I JUST DID AN EASY 10 MILES."

SORRY, **EASY?**

IF **10 MILES IS "EASY"**, what is **hard**? Running **until your bones dissolve?**

THE HOTDOG'S **Final Realization**

AFTER MONTHS OF **TRAINING, pain, and** questioning **my very existence**, I finally had a moment of clarity.

. . .

I WAS **NOT** A RUNNER.

I WAS **A HOTDOG.**

I WAS **NOT BUILT** for endurance sports. I was built for festivals, baseball games, and questionable decisions at gas stations.

I DID NOT NEED TO "PR." I did not need to "fuel up." I did not need **hydration tabs that cost more than my rent.**

SO I DID the only rational thing.

I STOPPED RUNNING.

AND I IMMEDIATELY **FELT BETTER.**

NOW, I wake up **pain-free.** My toenails are **still attached.** And the only marathon I participate in is **binge-watching bad reality TV.**

SO TO ALL the runners out there, I say:

.   .   .

GOOD FOR YOU.

ENJOY YOUR VO2 MAX. Enjoy your pacing. Enjoy waking up at **5 AM on a Sunday** to **run in the rain for fun.**

I'LL BE HERE. In my bun.

RESTING.

LIKE NATURE INTENDED.

FOUR

The Overachieving Wiener

A FIRST-PERSON NARRATIVE BY A WIENERMOBILE-WORTHY ATHLETE

"I was supposed to be just a snack. Now I'm a personality."

I was supposed to be **just a snack.**

MAYBE A CASUAL BARBECUE INDULGENCE. A fun ballpark treat. A late-night **questionable** gas station decision.

BUT NO.

SOMEWHERE ALONG THE WAY, I **bought a planner,** downloaded five productivity apps, and **became a high achiever.**

· · ·

NOW, I have a **personal brand.**

NOW, I **optimize my performance.**

NOW, **I hustle.**

THE PRODUCTIVITY CULT

IT STARTED INNOCENTLY ENOUGH.

I JUST WANTED to **be better.** Reach my full potential. Elevate myself **beyond the basic hotdogs** wasting their lives on cheap paper plates.

BUT HERE'S the thing about productivity: **Once you start, you can't stop.**

I FELL in with a **bad crowd**—the kind of people who listen to podcasts at **triple speed** and say things like:

"IF YOU'RE NOT WAKING *up at 4 AM, do you even WANT success?"*

. . .

THAT'S how I ended up in **the Productivity Cult.**

THESE PEOPLE DO NOT REST. They do not breathe. They do not casually enjoy a hotdog **at a barbecue like normal humans.**

EVERYTHING THEY DO IS part of **a larger strategy.**
- **Vacations?** A networking opportunity.
- **Hobbies?** Only if they generate income.
- **Eating lunch?** Only acceptable if it's "high-protein fuel" to "optimize output."

HOTDOGS ARE **LITERALLY FUEL.** But that's **not enough** for these people. They're out here eating chia seed pudding out of mason jars **at their standing desks**, acting like that's an acceptable way to live.

THE STUPID THINGS **Overachievers Say**

ONCE I STARTED PAYING ATTENTION, I realized that **overachievers are insane.**

1. **"I'll sleep when I'm dead."**

. . .

OH, **WILL YOU?**

BECAUSE IF YOU keep **ignoring sleep**, that's **coming up a lot sooner than you think.**

2. **"You have the same 24 hours as Elon Musk."**

OH, **DO I?**

I ALSO HAVE **one digestive tract, two functioning brain cells, and NO access** to an army of underpaid **employees** to handle my problems.

3. **"I wake up at 4 AM every day."**

THIS IS **NOT A BRAG.** This is **a medical concern.** If I wake up at 4 AM, it's because **I ate something questionable and my stomach is filing a complaint.**

4. "FAILURE IS NOT AN OPTION."

YES, it is. And if you don't believe me, come watch me try to do **one push-up.**

. . .

5. **"You should always be working toward something."**

I AM. It's called **digesting.**

THE LINKEDIN DISEASE

AT SOME POINT, **these people** stopped being normal and **became LinkedIn posts.**

YOU KNOW exactly the kind of post I'm talking about:
- **"This morning, I spilled coffee on myself before a big presentation. Instead of panicking, I remembered that great leaders turn setbacks into opportunities. I crushed the presentation. Lesson learned: BE ADAPTABLE."**
- **"When I was five, I sold lemonade for 25 cents a cup. Now I run a million-dollar startup. Success is a mindset."**
- **"I just worked 80 hours this week. No excuses. No breaks. Just hustle."**

SIR, *please go outside and touch some grass.*

. . .

WHEN SELF-IMPROVEMENT GOES TOO FAR

ONE DAY, I realized it had gone too far.

IT WAS **3 AM**. I was reading a **self-help book** titled *Crushing It: The 10X Guide to Maximum Efficiency*. I had a **daily gratitude journal, a high-performance morning routine**, and a **framed poster that said GRIND HARDER**.

I HADN'T **RELAXED** in months.

I HADN'T **EATEN a normal meal** without listening to an entrepreneurship podcast.

I WAS **BURNT OUT**.

BUT INSTEAD OF ACKNOWLEDGING IT, I did **what all overachievers do**—I **tried to optimize my burnout**.

"MAYBE IF I *wake up EVEN EARLIER and read FIVE self-improvement books instead of three, I'll get back on track.*"

. . .

THAT'S when I knew **I had become a monster.**

THE HOTDOG'S **Breaking Point**

THE FINAL STRAW came when I tried to **monetize my existence.**

YOU SEE, overachievers cannot **just exist.**

THEY MUST **BUILD A PERSONAL BRAND.**

AND SO, I did the unthinkable.

I **LAUNCHED A SIDE HUSTLE.**

I STARTED POSTING **thought leadership content.** I built a **funnel. I monetized my hobbies.**

THEN ONE DAY, someone invited me to a **"networking event"** and I realized **I had no idea what my own personality was anymore.**

· · ·

HAD I ever actually **liked** productivity? Or had I just **optimized myself into oblivion?**

I SAT DOWN. I took a deep breath. And for the first time in months, I asked myself:

WHAT IF I... **just relaxed?**

THE ANTI-HUSTLE **Revelation**

ONCE I QUIT, **I saw the truth.**

OVERACHIEVERS ARE **NOT HAPPY.**

THEY **PRETEND** THEY ARE. But deep down, they know:
- They haven't enjoyed a meal without **tracking their macros** in a decade.
- They don't actually **like networking**—they just think they should.
- They haven't experienced **joy** since they started scheduling it into their calendar.

THEY WAKE up **before the sun,** chug **something made of**

kale, listen to **a billionaire tell them to "crush it,"** and wonder why they feel empty inside.

THEY'RE JUST BURNT-OUT HOTDOGS.

THE HOTDOG'S **Final Decision**

SO I STOPPED.

I STOPPED **GRINDING.** I stopped **optimizing.** I stopped **waking up at 4 AM to write in a productivity journal.**

AND YOU KNOW WHAT?

NOTHING BAD HAPPENED.

IN FACT, my life **got better.**

NOW, I **sleep in.**

NOW, I **do things for fun.**

. . .

NOW, when someone tells me **"It's all about the hustle"**, I smile, take a deep breath, and say:

"NAH, I'M GOOD."

FIVE

The Midlife Crisis of a Footlong

A FIRST-PERSON NARRATIVE BY A HOTDOG WHO
PEAKED TOO SOON

"Why do people always pick the shorter ones? Is it because I'm too much commitment?"

It all started when someone called me a **"regular-sized hotdog."**

I LAUGHED it off at first. **Ha-ha, good one.** Obviously, I was **a footlong.** I had always been a **footlong.**

BUT THEN, I caught my reflection in a greasy napkin.

I LOOKED... smaller.

. . .

WERE MY ENDS **SHRIVELING?** Had my **bun expanded around me, making me look less impressive?** Was this why people were **ordering bratwursts instead of me?**

SUDDENLY, I knew what was happening.

I WAS HAVING A **MIDLIFE CRISIS.**

THE SIGNS **of a Midlife Crisis (According to a Hotdog)**

AT FIRST, I denied it. Midlife crises happen to **other hotdogs**—not me.

BUT THEN I started noticing the **classic warning signs.**

1. **Sudden Interest in Sports Cars**

ONE DAY, I was fine. The next, I was **Googling motorcycles** and wondering if a **footlong-sized convertible** existed.

2. **Weird New Hobbies**

· · ·

I DIDN'T JUST **START JOGGING**–I trained for a triathlon. I didn't just **get a tattoo**—I got one that said **"Live, Laugh, Grill."**

3. **Obsession with Looking Younger**

I CONSIDERED **BOTOX.** Then I remembered I **don't have a face.**

SO I STARTED USING **anti-aging condiments.**

"ORGANIC RELISH MAKES **you look five years younger."**

"MUSTARD IS FULL OF ANTIOXIDANTS."

"PROCESSED CHEESE CAUSES WRINKLES."

DID any of this make sense? **No.** But neither does **buying a sports car when you have two kids in college.**

WHEN YOU REALIZE **You're Not a Footlong**

. . .

IT HIT me at the worst possible moment.

I WAS AT A **BARBECUE**, standing proudly next to a **real** footlong.

THIS GUY WAS **HUGE**. A **stadium-grade beast. Double the girth. Perfect grill marks. The kind of hotdog that makes people say, "Whoa, I don't know if I can finish that."**

MEANWHILE, someone looked at me and said:

"OH GOOD, A NORMAL-SIZED ONE."

NORMAL-SIZED.

THAT WAS IT. My life was a **lie.**

THE FIVE STAGES **of a Midlife Crisis (According to a Hotdog)**

1. **Denial**

. . .

"THIS IS IMPOSSIBLE. *I'm a footlong. I've ALWAYS been a footlong.*"

I STARTED STANDING NEXT to **smaller hotdogs** to feel better. I **refused to take pictures** with bratwursts.

2. **Anger**

"WHY DOES *everyone else get to be bigger? Why do bratwursts get all the attention?*"

I STARTED **RESENTING CORN DOGS.**

"OH, **look at me, I have a crispy golden exterior. I'm so special.**"

SHUT UP, **Chad.**

3. **Bargaining**

"MAYBE IF I SWITCH BUNS, *I'll LOOK longer.*"

· · ·

I TRIED **LOW-CARB BUNS,** sesame seed buns, gluten-**free buns.** Nothing worked.

4. Depression

"WHY EVEN TRY? *I should just let myself get microwaved and accept my fate."*

I STARTED **HANGING** out in the back of the fridge, listening to **sad country music,** wondering if anyone would even notice if I disappeared.

5. Acceptance

"YOU KNOW WHAT? *Maybe size isn't everything."*

THIS WAS THE HARDEST PART. But eventually, I realized **there's more to life than being a footlong.**

THE HOTDOG WHO Tried Too Hard

THERE WAS one guy at the barbecue who had **the worst** midlife crisis I'd ever seen.

. . .

HE WAS **A CLASSIC HOTDOG**–JUST like me—but **refused to accept it.**

HE DID **EVERYTHING** TO OVERCOMPENSATE:
- Wore a pretzel bun to stand out.
- Got loaded up with every topping imaginable.
- Tried to pass himself off as an "artisan sausage."

AT FIRST, people **humored him.** They were like,

"OH, NICE, A FANCY HOTDOG."

BUT THEN REALITY SET IN.

YOU CAN **ADD ALL** the toppings you want, but deep down... you're **still a hotdog.**

AND IF YOU **try too hard** to be something you're not, people **will see right through it.**

THE HOTDOG'S **Final Realization**

. . .

I HAD to face the truth.

I WAS **NEVER** A FOOTLONG.

I WAS **ALWAYS A SIX-INCH.**

AND YOU KNOW WHAT? That's **okay.**

BECAUSE SOME PEOPLE **prefer six-inch hotdogs.** Some people **like a manageable portion.** Some people **don't want to commit to a whole footlong.**

I DIDN'T NEED a **sports car.** I didn't need **a new identity.**

I JUST NEEDED to be **the best six-inch hotdog I could be.**

SO I STEPPED FORWARD, embraced my size, and said:

"GRILL ME AS I AM."

AND IT WAS **the best barbecue of my life.**

SIX

The Barbecue Philosopher

A FIRST-PERSON NARRATIVE BY A HOTDOG WHO
HAS SEEN TOO MUCH

"If a hotdog is grilled but nobody is there to see it... am I still delicious?"

Every cookout has **one guy.**

YOU KNOW THE GUY.

THE **SELF-PROCLAIMED PITMASTER,** backyard guru, and philosopher of the flame.

TO HIM, **grilling isn't just cooking.** It's **an art form. A sacred tradition. A spiritual experience.**

AND HE WON'T JUST **GRILL** your food.

. . .

HE WILL GRILL YOUR MIND.

BECAUSE, you see, he's not **just making barbecue.** He's **dropping wisdom.** And somehow, **it always involves lighter fluid.**

THE BARBECUE PHILOSOPHER'S **Core Beliefs**

THE MOMENT he picks up those **oversized tongs,** he **transforms** into a philosopher. He speaks only in **metaphors, grilling proverbs, and unsolicited life advice.**

HERE ARE HIS **THREE COMMANDMENTS:**

1. **"You can tell a lot about a man by how he grills."**

NO, you can't. You can tell a lot about a man by **his tax records, his Google search history, or the fact that he calls his car 'The Beast.'**

2. "GRILLING IS LIFE."

.   .   .

I'M PRETTY sure **life is life.** But please, **continue comparing human existence to searing meat over open flames.**

3. "LIGHTER FLUID SOLVES EVERYTHING."

THIS IS THE BIG ONE.

THE BARBECUE PHILOSOPHER believes that **lighter fluid is the answer to all problems.**
- Fire won't start? **Lighter fluid.**
- Meat won't cook fast enough? **Lighter fluid.**
- Existential crisis? **Lighter fluid.**
- Flat tire? **Have you tried lighter fluid?**

THE MAN truly believes that **if you add enough lighter fluid to anything, it will either start working or burst into flames.**

WHICH, to be fair, is **not technically wrong.**

THE STUPID THINGS **Barbecue Philosophers Say**

.   .   .

AT SOME POINT, you'll be **trapped in a conversation with him.**

AND THAT'S when you realize: **This man believes he is the Aristotle of the Weber grill.**

1. "YOU GOTTA RESPECT THE MEAT."

OKAY, Greg. I'm literally **a hotdog.** What do you want me to do, **bow?**

2. **"Low and slow—that's how life should be."**

COOL, but my rent is due on the first and my boss **expects emails at the speed of light.**

3. "YOU CAN'T RUSH PERFECTION."

BUDDY, you **just ate a handful of shredded cheese straight from the bag,** let's not act like you're a Michelin-star chef.

4. **"Charcoal versus propane is like good versus evil."**

. . .

WHY IS THIS **A MORAL ISSUE?** Why are you acting like propane is **a war crime?**

5. **"This isn't just cooking—it's a conversation with the fire."**

THEN WHY IS the **fire actively trying to kill you?**

THE BBQ PHILOSOPHER'S "EXPERTISE" **on Life**

BECAUSE HE IS **SO good** at grilling, he assumes he is **good at everything else.**

HE WILL GIVE you **unhinged advice** on topics **he has no qualifications for.**

"RAISING KIDS? *It's like grilling ribs—low heat, lots of patience, and a little bit of sweet rub."*

"MARRIAGE? *That's just like flipping burgers. Do it too soon, and it falls apart."*

. . .

"INVESTING? *Same as smoking a brisket. You gotta wait it out, even when the stock market looks burnt.*"

SIR.

NOT EVERYTHING IS ABOUT BARBECUE.

THE OBSESSION **with Lighter Fluid**

AT FIRST, it's **just a tool.**

THEN, it becomes **a crutch.**

FINALLY, it becomes **his entire personality.**

IF SOMETHING IS **NOT ENGULFED** in flames **within five seconds,** this man will **absolutely drench it in lighter fluid.**

"MORE LIGHTER FLUID."
   "Just a splash more."
   "Alright, maybe one more splash."

"You know what? Screw it. Give me the whole bottle."

AT SOME POINT, you have to ask:

ARE WE GRILLING BURGERS, **or summoning a demon?**

THE HOTDOG'S **Breaking Point**

I PUT UP WITH IT. I listened to **his grilling philosophies, his unnecessary opinions on whiskey, his long rant about "real men only using charcoal."**

BUT THEN HE SAID IT.

THE **ONE PHRASE** that shattered me:

"HOTDOGS AREN'T REAL BARBECUE."

EXCUSE ME?

NOT REAL BARBECUE?

. . .

NOT REAL BARBECUE?

I HAVE BEEN to **every cookout,** every **tailgate,** every **backyard birthday party** since the dawn of time.

YOU THINK I'm **not real barbecue?**

SIR, I have **fed generations.**

I HAVE **BEEN THERE for America since the invention of the grill.**

MEANWHILE, your brisket takes **14 hours** and tastes like **a leather shoe soaked in disappointment.**

THE HOTDOG'S **Final Revelation**

I REALIZED something important that day.

THE BARBECUE PHILOSOPHER isn't **really** about barbecue.

. . .

HE'S ABOUT **CONTROL.**

HIS ENTIRE PERSONALITY is **being the guy at the grill.** It makes him feel **wise, powerful, essential.**

WITHOUT IT, he's just **another guy at the cookout.**

AND THAT'S when I understood:

SOMETIMES, **a man doesn't need wisdom.**
   Sometimes, he just needs an apron that says "Grill Sergeant" and a gallon of lighter fluid.

AND HONESTLY?

THAT'S OKAY.

BECAUSE IN THE END, the grill is hot, the food is good, and as long as he doesn't **burn down the garage**, we'll all get fed.

EVEN ME.

SEVEN

The Relish Rebellion

A FIRST-PERSON NARRATIVE BY A HOTDOG WATCHING GREEN CONDIMENTS LOSE THEIR MINDS

"Why does relish get treated like an afterthought? I'm tired of living in mustard's shadow!"

I always knew relish was a little **off.**

MAYBE IT WAS the **unnatural neon-green glow.** Maybe it was the **way it sat in the jar, all chopped up and unhinged, waiting to be spooned onto unsuspecting hotdogs.**

BUT I NEVER IMAGINED **THEY'D start a revolution.**

AND YET, here we are.

. . .

THE **RELISH REBELLION** is in full swing, and buddy, let me tell you—these guys are **serious.**

THEY CLAIM the world is **overpopulated.** That **hotdogs are destroying the planet.** That if we don't **take drastic action right now,** it's all over.

AND TO BE CLEAR—I'M **not** against taking care of the planet. I'm literally made of **mystery meat and industrialized food production.** I know we've got problems.

BUT **THESE GUYS?**

THEY'RE **ABSOLUTELY INSANE.**

THE MANIFESTO **of the Relish Rebellion**

THE LEADER OF THE MOVEMENT, **Brother Picklestein,** has written an **800-page manifesto** (that nobody read) outlining their core beliefs.

HERE'S THE SHORT VERSION:

. . .

1. **There Are Too Many Hotdogs**

ACCORDING TO THE RELISH REBELLION, the world is facing a **hotdog overpopulation crisis.** There are simply **too many of us** being consumed at **an unsustainable rate.**

THEIR SOLUTION?

"WE NEED TO REDUCE PRODUCTION! **DECREASE consumption! FIGHT back against the capitalist sausage-industrial complex!"**

MEANWHILE, I'm sitting here thinking...

BUDDY, **I don't think anyone's out here hoarding hotdogs.**

THE ONLY TIME there's **too many hotdogs** is when someone forgets to buy the right bun-to-dog ratio.

2. **Only Sustainable Toppings Should Be Allowed**

. . .

THE REBELLION **HATES** PROCESSED CONDIMENTS.
- Ketchup? **Too much sugar.**
- Mustard? **Tied to colonial history, somehow.**
- Cheese? **An environmental disaster.**
- Bacon bits? **A crime against nature.**

THEIR **IDEAL HOTDOG** IS A **VEGAN,** gluten-free, air-fried, ethically-sourced plant tube topped with **locally foraged moss.**

YUM.

3. **Drastic Measures Must Be Taken IMMEDIATELY**

THERE'S NO **NEGOTIATION**. No middle ground. No incentives to encourage better behavior.

THE ONLY SOLUTION IS **RADICAL, top-down control.**

THEY HAVE **no plan for how normal people** are supposed to live under their new rules.

BUT THEY DON'T CARE.

· · ·

BECAUSE THEY HAVE **a spreadsheet that proves they're right.**

THE PROBLEM **With Top-Down Thinking**

THE **RELISH REBELLION** operates on **one major assumption:**

IF **we just force people to comply, everything will be fine.**

THIS IS **the dumbest assumption possible.**

HAS **FORCING** people to do things ever worked?
- **Prohibition?** People drank anyway.
- **The Metric System?** America said **nah.**
- **Movie theaters banning outside snacks?** *Nice try, Greg, but my hoodie pockets are filled with M&Ms.*

IF YOU WANT **REAL CHANGE,** you need to **give people a reason to care.**

BECAUSE LET'S BE HONEST–**NOBODY** does anything unless there's an incentive.

• You want people to drive electric cars? **Make them cheaper than gas cars.**

• You want people to recycle? **Make it worth their time.**

• You want people to use less energy? **Give them a discount for it.**

BUT THE **RELISH Rebellion** doesn't believe in incentives.

THEY BELIEVE IN **RULES,** regulations, and scolding people.

WHICH MEANS their movement is **doomed to fail.**

HOW THE RELISH **Rebellion Would Flounder in a Good Future**

THE FUNNIEST POSSIBLE OUTCOME?

WHAT IF **EVERYTHING** turns out fine?

• What if new technology solves the energy crisis?

• What if lab-grown meat becomes **cheap and delicious?**

• What if we fix climate change **without collapsing society?**

. . .

THE RELISH REBELLION **would lose their minds.**

BECAUSE THEY **NEED** **the world to be doomed.**

THEIR ENTIRE PERSONALITY is based on **yelling at people for killing the planet.**

IF WE **ACTUALLY SOLVE THE** **problem**, what are they supposed to do?

THE RETURN **to Malthusian Relish**

LET'S say the world **doesn't collapse.**

LET'S say everything **gets better.**

WOULD the Relish Rebellion **admit they were wrong?**

OF COURSE NOT.

. . .

THEY'D JUST **PIVOT** to a new crisis.

INSTEAD OF YELLING ABOUT **OVERPOPULATION**, they'd start yelling about **"over-sustainability."**

THEY'D CLAIM that we've **gone too far** and that people are now **too comfortable.**

THEY'D PUSH for a **return to simpler times—back when life was hard and food was scarce.**

THEY'D REBRAND themselves as **Malthusian Relish.**

THEIR SLOGAN?

"SUFFERING BUILDS CHARACTER."

BECAUSE DEEP DOWN, the **Relish Rebellion** isn't really about **saving the world.**

IT'S about **being miserable** and making sure **everyone else is, too.**

. . .

THE HOTDOG'S **Final Verdict**

LOOK, I get it. The world **has problems.** Climate change is **real**. We **should** take care of the planet.

BUT **FORCING** people to comply with impossible rules isn't the answer.

IF YOU ACTUALLY WANT CHANGE, **make sustainability profitable.**

BECAUSE WHEN **SELF-INTEREST** lines up with **good policy**, things actually happen.

THAT'S **NOT IDEAL**. But it's **realistic.**

AND THAT'S MORE than I can say for the **Relish Rebellion.**

NOW, if you'll excuse me, I'm going to sit back, enjoy my (non-vegan) bun, and watch these guys fight each other over **whether free-range mustard is ethical.**

EIGHT

The Fast Food Family Reunion

A FIRST-PERSON NARRATIVE BY A HOTDOG
SURROUNDED BY GREASE AND GENETIC CHAOS

"Burgers get all the fame, but who kept summer cookouts alive? Me."

If there's one thing I've learned in this life, it's that **fast food people and family reunion people are the same species.**

THEY THRIVE IN **CROWDED,** chaotic environments. They **love** cheap, overly processed food. They **think anything that happened in the past is automatically "the best."**

AND ABOVE ALL ELSE, **they don't believe in personal space.**

THE "FAST FOOD PEOPLE" **Phenomenon**

. . .

SOME PEOPLE **ENJOY** FAST FOOD.

BUT THEN THERE are **Fast Food People.**

THESE PEOPLE DON'T JUST **EAT** FAST food. They **worship** it.
- They refer to McDonald's as **"Mickey D's" like it's their best friend.**
- They have **a preferred Taco Bell location** because "the other one doesn't do the sauce right."
- They think **Burger King is underrated** and will fight you about it.
- They **refuse to acknowledge** that Subway is just **a sandwich lottery.**

IF YOU TELL them fast food is **unhealthy,** they'll **laugh in your face** while dipping their fries into a **McFlurry like a lunatic.**

THE UNHOLY UNION **of Fast Food and Family Reunions**

NOW, take a **Fast Food Person** and **drop them into a family reunion.**

. . .

CONGRATULATIONS.

YOU HAVE **CREATED** an unstoppable force of loud opinions, cheap food, and unsolicited advice about your life.

FAMILY REUNIONS ARE **JUST** like fast food:
- **Overhyped.** (Everyone says it'll be "so much fun," but by the second hour, you're praying for a meteor strike.)
- **Way too greasy.** (Someone's uncle always brings a plate of ribs that could be used to lube an engine.)
- **Filled with regret.** (By the end, you feel physically and emotionally drained, questioning every decision that led you here.)

THE STUPID THINGS **People Say at Family Reunions**

AT SOME POINT, someone will say **one of these classic reunion lines.**

1. **"I haven't seen you since you were this big!"**

GREAT. I have **also not seen you since I was "this big."** That's **how time works.**

.   .   .

2. "ARE YOU STILL SINGLE?"

NO, actually, I've been in a **beautiful, committed relationship with avoiding this conversation.**

3. **"We should do this every year!"**

NO, we should **absolutely not.**

4. **"You need to eat more! You look too thin!"**

I AM **A LITERAL HOTDOG**. My entire existence is **edible.** What more do you want from me?

5. **"You remind me of your father."**

OH? You mean the man who **fled this exact reunion 20 years ago and was never seen again?** Cool, thanks.

THE WEIRD COUSINS **& Unhinged Family Dynamics**

.   .   .

EVERY FAMILY REUNION has **the same types of people.**

THE ONE COUSIN **Who Thinks They're a Big Deal**

THEY **MOVED TO A CITY.** They have **a podcast.** They **brought a bottle of wine** and will spend the whole reunion explaining why **it's better than your beer.**

THE UNCLE **Who Hasn't Sat Down in 20 Years**

WHY IS HE **ALWAYS PACING?** Does he think **someone is watching him?** What **war crime** did he commit that prevents him from **resting his legs for more than two minutes?**

THE AUNT **Who Pretends She Loves Everybody**

SHE WILL **HUG YOU AGGRESSIVELY,** tell you how much she loves you, and then immediately **go talk trash about you to another aunt.**

THE KID **That Nobody Knows**

. . .

EVERY REUNION HAS **a random kid that no one can place.**

"WHOSE CHILD IS THAT?"
   "No idea. Just let him play in the yard and hope he goes home with the right people."

THE CONSPIRACY THEORY **Grandpa**

AT SOME POINT, **he will find you.** And he will **drop some knowledge.**
   • **"The moon landing was staged."**
   • **"The government controls the weather."**
   • **"Fast food used to be better before they started putting chemicals in the buns."**

BRO. **We are literally eating gas station hamburgers right now.** The **buns are the least of our problems.**

THE FEAR **of Romantic Incidents at Family Reunions**

LISTEN.

.   .   .

NOBODY **WANTS** to talk about it.

BUT EVERY FAMILY reunion **has at least one situation that gets a little too... Alabama.**

SOMEWHERE, deep in the crowd of people who **only see each other once every ten years,** there are two people who are **flirting just a little too much.**

AND NOBODY KNOWS if they're actually related.

SOME PEOPLE WILL **LAUGH** it off.
Some people will **look the other way.**
But deep down, **everyone is praying they check the family tree before** taking things any further.

THE TRAGEDY OF FAST FOOD **& Reunion Culture**

THE **FAST FOOD** lover and the **family reunion fanatic** are, tragically, the same person.
• They **romanticize the past** and refuse to believe things have changed.
• They believe **grease is a food group.**
• They **cling to bad traditions** out of sheer stubbornness.

. . .

"BACK IN MY DAY, *Burger King had the best fries.*"
 "*Back in my day, family meant something.*"

BACK IN YOUR DAY, **people died from eating expired mayonnaise.**

LET'S not pretend **the past was perfect.**

THE HOTDOG'S **Final Verdict**

I GET IT.

FAST FOOD **IS COMFORTING**. Family reunions **have their moments.** But let's be real—

NEITHER OF THESE **things should be treated like a religion.**

AT SOME POINT, you have to **accept reality.**
 • Fast food **is what it is.** It's delicious, terrible for you, and **not the same as it was in 1998.**
 • Family reunions are **a survival exercise.** You don't

go to have fun. **You go to make sure nobody in your family is secretly dating their cousin.**

AND IN THE END, that's the best we can hope for.

NOW, if you'll excuse me, I need to escape **before someone starts calling me** "little hotdog" **and pinching my bun.**

NINE

The Sausage Ancestry Test

A FIRST-PERSON NARRATIVE BY A HOTDOG
CONFRONTING SOME HARD TRUTHS

"Turns out I'm 12% bratwurst, 25% chorizo, and 63% mystery meat. I have so many questions."

I always thought I was just **a regular hotdog.**

NOTHING FANCY. Just **meat, bun, and a slightly mysterious past.**

THEN I TOOK a **Sausage Ancestry Test.**

AND EVERYTHING **CHANGED.**

THE IDENTITY CRISIS **of a Sausage**

. . .

YOU SEE, hotdogs don't just **come from one place.**

WE ARE **a glorious mixture of questionable origins. A genetic smoothie of meats. A delicious mystery wrapped in a casing that nobody should ask too many questions about.**

BUT THAT'S the thing about ancestry tests.

THEY DON'T LET you **lie to yourself.**

SO WHEN I spat into that tiny tube (which was difficult, considering I don't have a mouth), I had **no idea** what kind of existential nightmare I was about to unlock.

THE DNA RESULTS: "IT'S COMPLICATED"

A FEW WEEKS LATER, the results came in.

I OPENED THE EMAIL, expecting something **simple and clean.** Maybe **80% beef, 20% pork.**

INSTEAD, I got this:

- 12% Bratwurst
- 15% Chorizo
- 9% Andouille
- 7% Kielbasa
- 19% Mystery Meat (Government Sealed)
- 3% Hot Pocket Filling
- 0.04% Lobster Roll??

I WASN'T JUST **one thing.**

I WAS A **SAUSAGE MELTING POT.** A **CULINARY MUTT.** A frankfurter Frankenstein.

WHO WAS I?

AND MORE IMPORTANTLY– **WHY** was there lobster in me?

THE HARD TRUTH: **Evolution is Messy**

AT THIS POINT, I had two choices:

1. **Accept the reality** that hotdogs, like all sausages, have **a long, complex history of adaptation, mixture, and evolution.**

2. **Deny reality** and insist that I was **100% purebred**

footlong, placed on this Earth exactly as I am, 6,000 years ago.

GUESS which one a lot of sausages go with?

THE SAUSAGES **Who Don't Believe in Evolution**

THERE'S a **certain type of sausage** that **does not want to hear about ancestry.**

THESE ARE THE **FUNDAMENTALIST FRANKS.**

THE ONES WHO BELIEVE THAT:
 • **Hotdogs were created exactly as they are today, with no mixing of meats.**
 • **There is no evidence that bratwursts and kielbasa share a common ancestor.**
 • **The Earth is only 6,000 years old, and all sausages existed in their current form since the beginning of time.**

BUDDY.

. . .

OUR **ENTIRE EXISTENCE** is based on blending meats together.

WE **LITERALLY** EVOLVED into this form by taking **bits of everything and making something new.**

BUT THESE GUYS **won't hear it.**

"I DON'T COME *from chorizo! That's a LIE made up by Big Meat Science!"*

SIR.

YOUR **ENTIRE FAMILY** tree is made of leftovers.

THE STUPID THINGS **Fundamentalist Sausages Say**

ONCE YOU START ARGUING with these guys, you realize something:

THEY HAVE **no idea how science works.**

. . .

1. **"If hotdogs evolved from bratwursts, why are there still bratwursts?"**

OH MY SWEET, clueless frankfurter.

WE **DIDN'T REPLACE** BRATWURSTS. We **branched off from them.** Just like how **humans didn't replace monkeys.** We all **share an ancestor.**

EVOLUTION IS **NOT A LADDER.** It's a messy, sausage-filled family tree.

2. **"There's no way we all come from the same meat!"**

BUDDY. **Look at our ingredients.** We are all **the same collection of animal parts, spices, and preservatives, just arranged in slightly different ways.**

WE'RE **like the regional dialects of meat.**
- In Germany, we became **bratwurst.**
- In Poland, we became **kielbasa.**
- In Mexico, we became **chorizo.**
- In America, we became **a hotdog that legally can't be called "meat" without an asterisk.**

. . .

3. "THERE ARE NO TRANSITIONAL SAUSAGES!"

OH REALLY? **Then explain the existence of the Cheddarwurst.**

OR THE **TURKEY DOG.**

OR **WHATEVER UNHOLY HYBRID** Taco Bell is working on right now.

WE ARE **ALWAYS EVOLVING.**

YOU'RE EATING THE EVIDENCE.

THE FEAR OF BEING "MIXED"

AT THE CORE OF IT, **some sausages just don't want to accept that they're a mixture.**

THEY WANT to believe they are **pure, untouched, untainted.**

. . .

BUT HERE'S THE THING—

NOTHING IS PURE.

EVERYTHING IS a **combination of what came before it.**

AND **FIGHTING** that reality just makes you look **ridiculous.**

IMAGINE A HOTDOG SAYING:

"I AM A PURE, **100% ORIGINAL** hotdog. **No** outside **influences."**

SIR.

YOU ARE MADE from **at least four different animals and one ingredient that was banned in Europe.**

YOU HAVE the **genetic history of a casserole.**

YOU ARE **MEAT DUCT TAPE.**

. . .

ACCEPT IT.

THE HOTDOG'S **Final Realization**

AFTER WEEKS OF **DENIAL,** panic Googling, and **one very embarrassing argument with a bratwurst on Twitter,** I finally came to terms with my ancestry.

I WAS **NOT** A PUREBRED HOTDOG.

I WAS **A MIX OF EVERYTHING.**

AND HONESTLY?

THAT MADE ME **BETTER.**

BECAUSE BEING **a mixture** means that I have **history.** That I have **depth.** That I am **the result of generations of adaptation and improvement.**

I AM NOT **LESSER** because I'm made of different things.

. . .

I AM **MORE**.

AND THAT'S a **beautiful** thing to accept.

NOW, if you'll excuse me, I have to go explain to a group of sausages that **carbon dating is real and ketchup did not ride dinosaurs.**

TEN

The Hotdog Who Wanted to Be a Taco

A FIRST-PERSON NARRATIVE BY A HOTDOG WHO JUST WANTS TO BE LOVED

"They said I couldn't. They said I shouldn't. But I believe in myself."

You ever feel like you were **born into the wrong food category?**

LIKE, maybe **you're a hotdog,** but deep down, **you feel like you were meant to be something else?**

SOMETHING... spicier?

SOMETHING... a little more **exciting?**

. . .

SOMETHING... **that women actually want to order?**

BECAUSE LET ME TELL YOU–**WOMEN** love tacos.

TACOS ARE **THE COOL,** charming, mysterious foreigner.

Hotdogs? We're **the guy she settles for when the taco place is closed.**

AND BUDDY, I have had **enough of it.**

THE FEMININE HOTDOG **Struggle**

I DON'T KNOW when it started, but at some point in my life, I realized that **women don't respect hotdogs.**

THEY LIKE US **IRONICALLY**.
- They'll eat us at **barbecues** because **it's convenient.**
- They'll order us at **sporting events** because **there are no better options.**
- They'll take a picture of us at a **4th of July cookout** for **the nostalgia factor.**

BUT DO THEY **CRAVE US?**

. . .

DO THEY **ROMANTICIZE US?**

DO they tell their friends how much they love a good hotdog?

ABSOLUTELY NOT.

TACOS, **though?**

TACOS HAVE GROUPIES.

WOMEN **LITERALLY SCHEDULE "TACO TUESDAYS."** Entire days of the week are dedicated to them.

NO ONE HAS EVER SAID, **"Let's go out for hotdogs!"**

I WANTED **THAT LIFE.** I wanted that kind of love.

SO I MADE A DECISION.

. . .

I WAS GOING to **become a taco.**

THE HOTDOG-TO-TACO TRANSFORMATION

I STARTED **CHANGING EVERYTHING.**
- **I got spicier.** I started **rolling with jalapeños.**
- **I upgraded my toppings.** No more **cheap mustard** —only guacamole, pico de gallo, and artisanal salsa.
- **I worked on my presentation.** No more **basic buns** —only soft, warm tortillas.

I WASN'T JUST **a hotdog anymore.**

I WAS **HOTDOG 2.0.**

A **LATIN FUSION EXPERIENCE.**

I THOUGHT **this would fix everything.**

I THOUGHT **women would finally see me differently.**

I WAS **WRONG.**

· · ·

THE WOMEN **in My Life Had Some Thoughts**

MY GIRLFRIEND'S **Response**

"WHY ARE YOU TRYING SO HARD?"

BECAUSE I **WANT** to be desirable.

BECAUSE I **WANT** to be chosen first.

BECAUSE I **WANT** to be devoured with enthusiasm, not as an afterthought.

"I LIKED you better when you weren't trying to be something you're not."

OH.

WELL, that's **annoying.**

MY FEMALE FRIENDS' **Response**

. . .

"YOU'RE ACTING DIFFERENT. **Just be a hotdog.**"

I AM A HOTDOG.

THAT'S THE PROBLEM.

"WE LOVE HOTDOGS! **Just, you know… not in the way you think.**"

OUCH.

THAT'S LIKE SAYING, **"You have such a great personality."**

THAT'S **women's way of saying, "I would never date you, but I hope you're available to move my furniture."**

MY MOM'S **Response**

"WHY ARE **you acting like this? You were raised better."**

. . .

GREAT. Now my **own mother** was implying that my tortilla phase was an embarrassment to the family.

"YOU'RE STILL MY SON, **but I can't pretend this isn't weird."**

I DIDN'T ASK for **this intervention.**

WHY WOMEN LIKE **Tacos More Than Hotdogs**

AT SOME POINT, I had to face the truth.

IT WASN'T about **the spice.** It wasn't about **the toppings.**

TACOS JUST HAD **something I didn't.**
* **Tacos are "exotic."** (Even though they're literally everywhere now.)
* **Tacos are "fun."** (Which is apparently different from "stupid fun," which is what hotdogs are.)
* **Tacos have "culture."** (Okay, fair, but do you think I *chose* to be a processed meat tube?)

WOMEN LOVE **tacos** because tacos **play the game better.**

. . .

MEANWHILE, I was trying to **earn respect** instead of **demanding it.**

BIG MISTAKE.

THE TRAGEDY **of the Feminine Hotdog**

YOU KNOW what's worse than being **rejected?**

BEING **LIKED,** but never desired.

BEING **"A NICE OPTION,"** but never "the best choice."

WOMEN WANT **TACOS.** They want **steaks.** They want **sushi.**

HOTDOGS? We're **the guy they friend-zone.**

WE'RE **the guy they say is so funny and kind, but never the one they date.**

AND THE **WORST PART?**

. . .

WHEN YOU **TRY** to be more exciting, they **call you weird.**

SO I WAS STUCK.

THE HOTDOG'S **Final Realization**

I HAD A CHOICE.

I COULD **KEEP TRYING** to be a taco and lose what little respect I had left.

OR...

I COULD JUST **BE the best damn hotdog I could be.**

BECAUSE LET'S BE HONEST–
- Hotdogs **are dependable.**
- Hotdogs **never let you down.**
- Hotdogs **are always there when you need them.**

MAYBE I'LL NEVER BE a **sexy taco.**

. . .

MAYBE I'LL ALWAYS BE the **casual, convenient, nostalgic option.**

BUT YOU KNOW WHAT?

PEOPLE **ALWAYS COME BACK** to hotdogs.

AND **THAT'S** good enough for me.

NOW, if you'll excuse me, I need to go stand confidently in my bun and accept my fate.

ELEVEN

The Vegan Hotdog Impostor

A FIRST-PERSON NARRATIVE BY A HOTDOG WHO KNOWS WHAT REAL FOOD IS

"I'm totally meat. Definitely. No need to check the ingredients, haha."

There's a **vegan hotdog** at this barbecue.

I KNOW, I know. **I didn't think they existed either.**

BUT HERE HE IS, standing next to me like we're **the same.**

WE ARE NOT THE SAME.

BECAUSE I AM **REAL FOOD.**

. . .

AND HE?

HE IS A FRAUD.

THE TRAGEDY **of the Vegan Hotdog**

THE FIRST THING you need to know about **vegan hotdogs** is that **nobody actually wants them.**

- **Vegans don't want them.** They just pretend to because they **miss real hotdogs.**
- **Meat eaters don't want them.** Because **why would we?**
- **Even the vegan hotdog doesn't want to be a vegan hotdog.**

YOU EVER SEEN one in a grocery store? **They look ashamed to exist.**

THEY TRY to **dress it up** in fancy packaging:
- **"Plant-Based Frankfurter!"**
- **"Sustainable Sausage!"**
- **"Guilt-Free Grillers!"**

BUDDY.

. . .

YOU ARE NOT A SAUSAGE. You are **a sadness tube.**

THE LIES **of the Vegan Hotdog**

THE WORST PART?

THIS GUY IS **TRYING** to pass himself off as one of us.

"NO, **bro, I taste just like the real thing."**

OH?

DO YOU?

YOU TASTE **JUST LIKE** A HOTDOG?

BECAUSE I TOOK **one bite of you, and now my mouth tastes like a yoga mat and broken dreams.**

THE VEGAN ARGUMENT: "MEAT IS UNNECESSARY"

· · ·

VEGAN HOTDOGS ARE part of a **larger conspiracy**—one that says humans **don't need meat to survive.**

WHICH IS HILARIOUS.

BECAUSE **EVERYTHING** great about civilization started with meat.

THINK ABOUT IT.

THE HUNTER-GATHERER GOLDEN **Age**

ONCE UPON A TIME, men were **gods.**
- They **hunted mammoths.**
- They **grilled over open flames.**
- They **drank mead out of skulls.**
- They **invented tools, society, and problem-solving.**

AND WHY?

BECAUSE THEY **ATE MEAT.**

. . .

PROTEIN **BUILT THEIR MUSCLES**. Fire cooked their food. And alcohol made them philosophical.

THIS WAS the **golden age of masculinity.**

THESE WERE the guys who **built empires, fought wars, and solved real problems.**

MEANWHILE, the **vegetarian population** was... well...

THE LOTUS EATERS: **The Original Vegans**

YOU EVER READ **THE ODYSSEY**?

THERE'S a part where Odysseus finds **a group of people who just sit around all day, eating plants, doing nothing, thinking about nothing.**

THEY'RE CALLED **the Lotus Eaters.**

AND GUESS WHAT?

. . .

THAT'S **what happens when you don't eat meat.**
- No ambition.
- No fire.
- No innovation.
- Just **chewing on leaves and vibing.**

THESE WERE **NOT** the men who built pyramids.

THESE WERE **NOT** the men who discovered electricity.

THESE WERE the men who said, **"Eh, maybe tomorrow,"** and then **went back to eating their stupid plants.**

THE VEGAN PLAN: **Bugs and Lab Goo**

THE **REAL PLAN** isn't just to take away meat.

IT'S to **replace it** with something **far worse.**

AND GUESS **what's on the menu?**

1. **Eating Bugs**

• • •

"CRICKETS ARE A SUSTAINABLE PROTEIN SOURCE!"

OKAY, **so is beef.**

YOU KNOW WHAT **COWS EAT?** Grass. The most **abundant** thing on Earth.

BUT NO–**THEY** want you to eat insects.

BECAUSE **NOTHING SAYS "THRIVING SOCIETY"** like chugging a cockroach smoothie.

2. **Lab-Grown Mystery Meat**

"IT'S JUST LIKE REAL BEEF!"

COOL. Then **you eat it.**

I'M NOT interested in **a steak that was 3D-printed in a Petri dish.**

3. **Soy Everything**

. . .

"SOY PROTEIN IS JUST **as good as real protein."**

OH REALLY?

THEN WHY DO men who eat **too much soy** start looking like they should be **playing the flute in a Renaissance festival?**

THE HOTDOG'S **Final Realization**

LOOK, I'm not against **eating plants.**

I LOVE **VEGETABLES.**

THEY SIT **on the side of my steak, looking pretty.**

BUT LET'S not **rewrite history.**

MEAT MADE **CIVILIZATION.**

. . .

MEAT BUILT **WARRIORS,** thinkers, and inventors.

MEAT IS **why we're here.**

AND I WILL **NEVER** APOLOGIZE for that.

NOW, if you'll excuse me, I need to go stand next to the grill before someone tries to replace me with a cricket burrito.

TWELVE

The Final Bite

A FIRST-PERSON NARRATIVE BY A HOTDOG WHO
HAS SEEN TOO MUCH

"We all know our fate. But until then... let's be delicious."

Well, here we are.

THE **END OF THE ROAD.**

THE LAST BITE.

THE FINAL MOMENT before **someone dunks me in
mustard and finishes me off.**

I'VE SEEN A LOT. **I've learned a lot.** And before I go, I
want to share **one last reflection on life, existence, and
the absolute nonsense that is the world of hotdogs.**

. . .

SO LET'S take a moment to **look back** at everything we've been through.

BECAUSE BUDDY– **IT'S been a ride.**

WHAT I'VE LEARNED **from a Life as a Hotdog**

IF THERE'S one thing I know for sure, it's this:

PEOPLE ARE INSANE.

I MEAN, truly.

I HAVE **WITNESSED CONSPIRACIES,** existential crises, overachievers, midlife breakdowns, barbecue philosophers, environmental zealots, weird family reunions, confused sausages, insecure hotdogs, vegan imposters, and a society actively trying to replace real food with crickets.

AND YET, **somehow, the world keeps turning.**

. . .

HERE'S what I've learned from **each chapter of my absurd, processed existence.**

1. **The Ketchup Conspiracy: The World is Run by Questionable People**

REMEMBER when I discovered that **Big Mustard might be running a smear campaign against ketchup?**

THAT WAS my first introduction to the **truth about the world.**

EVERYTHING IS A CONSPIRACY TO SOMEONE.

IF A DECISION DOESN'T MAKE sense, follow the money.

If someone argues too passionately about condiments, don't trust them.

If a man in a trench coat starts whispering about "the condiment elite," it's time to leave the cookout.

2. **The Existential Bun Crisis: Nobody Knows What They Are**

WE ARE ALL **LOST HOTDOGS.**

. . .

AM I A SANDWICH? Am I a taco? Am I something **more?**

DOES IT MATTER?

PROBABLY NOT.

BECAUSE AT THE end of the day, **labels are stupid.**

THE BUN DOESN'T DEFINE you.
The toppings don't define you.
You define you.

AND IF THAT sounds like something **a self-help guru would put on a throw pillow—good.**

MAYBE **THEY'RE RIGHT** for once.

3. **The Hotdog Marathoner: People Love Making Their Lives Harder**

HERE'S the thing about **runners.**

. . .

THEY AREN'T RUNNING **for survival.** They aren't running **from danger.**

THEY'RE JUST RUNNING... **to run.**

SOME PEOPLE DON'T KNOW how to sit still.

Some people need their suffering to be **self-inflicted.**

Some people think losing toenails makes them stronger.

I **DO NOT UNDERSTAND** these people.

BUT I RESPECT THEM. From **a distance.**

A VERY, **very** far distance.

4. **The Overachieving Wiener: Productivity is a Disease**

SOME PEOPLE **WAKE** up at 4 AM, drink a protein shake made of regret, and start "crushing it" before the sun even rises.

. . .

AND TO THOSE PEOPLE, I say:

WHY?

WORK IS FINE. Hustle culture is a mental illness.
    If you burn out, nobody will thank you.
    Sometimes the best thing to do is **literally nothing.**

AND IF THAT BOTHERS YOU, maybe ask yourself: **Who are you working this hard for?**

5. **The Midlife Crisis of a Footlong: Acceptance is Freedom**

I SPENT an **embarrassing amount of time** trying to convince myself I was a footlong.

BUT DEEP DOWN, I always knew the truth.

I'M A SIX-INCH.

. . .

AND YOU KNOW WHAT?

THAT'S OKAY.

YOU DON'T NEED to be bigger.
You don't need a sports car.
You don't need a tattoo that says "Live, Laugh, Grill."

YOU JUST NEED to **accept what you are and be proud of it.**

6. **The Barbecue Philosopher: Just Because You Can Grill Doesn't Mean You Know Everything**

SOME MEN GAIN **control of a grill and suddenly believe they are Plato.**

THESE PEOPLE ARE **DANGEROUS.**

NOT EVERYTHING IS ABOUT LIGHTER fluid.
Not everything is a metaphor for "real life."
Sometimes a hotdog is just a hotdog.

. . .

AND SOMETIMES, the best thing you can do is **nod, smile, and let them rant about charcoal.**

7. **The Relish Rebellion: People Love Telling Other People What to Do**

IF THERE'S one thing I've learned, it's that **every generation** has a group of people **who want to control everything.**

THEY ARE ALWAYS CONVINCED the world is ending.

They are always convinced that **they alone** have the solution.

They are always **deeply annoying.**

THE TRUTH?

THE WORLD IS PROBABLY GOING **to be fine.**

AND IF IT ISN'T?

WELL, at least I won't be around to see it.

. . .

8. **The Fast Food Family Reunion: Nostalgia is a Scam**

FAST FOOD USED to be better.

FAMILY USED TO BE CLOSER.

THE PAST WAS **SO AMAZING.**

EXCEPT...

IT WASN'T.
   You just forgot all the terrible parts.
   Time makes **everything seem better than it was.**

SO MAYBE INSTEAD OF **chasing the past,** we just **make the present better.**

CRAZY IDEA, I know.

9. **The Sausage Ancestry Test: Nobody is Pure**

.   .   .

I LEARNED that I'm **12% bratwurst, 9% chorizo, and 3% something labeled "government-classified."**

AND THAT'S OKAY.

EVERYONE COMES FROM SOMEWHERE.
Nobody is 100% anything.
If you think you are, you probably just haven't taken a DNA test yet.

SAUSAGES ARE **GENETIC SMOOTHIES.**

AND **SO IS HUMANITY.**

DEAL WITH IT.

10. **The Hotdog Who Wanted to Be a Taco: Attraction is Unfair**

WOMEN **LOVE TACOS.**

WOMEN DO **NOT** LOVE HOTDOGS.

.   .   .

YOU CAN REINVENT YOURSELF, but people will still see what they want to see.

Being the "nice, safe option" sucks, but you can't force people to want you.

At some point, you just have to be **okay with what you are.**

BESIDES–**HOTDOGS** always make a comeback.

WE MIGHT NOT BE **the first choice, but we're never fully forgotten.**

11. **The Vegan Hotdog Imposter: Meat is Life**

THE **ENTIRE COURSE** of human civilization was built on fire, meat, and problem-solving.

AND NOW THEY want us to **eat bugs?**

NO.

Absolutely not.

I refuse.

MEAT BUILT THE WORLD.

. . .

AND I, for one, **am not going to apologize for it.**

THE FINAL LESSON: **Enjoy the Bite While You Can**

AT THE END of the day, what have I learned?

LIFE IS RIDICULOUS.

PEOPLE ARE **WEIRD**. Society is **a mess.** Nobody knows **what's going on.**

BUT THAT'S FINE.

BECAUSE **WE'RE ALL** in this together.

SO MY FINAL ADVICE?

LAUGH AT THE NONSENSE.
    Question everything.
    Accept what you are.
    And never—**never**—let anyone tell you to eat a vegan

hotdog.

NOW, if you'll excuse me, it's time for **the final bite.**

AND BUDDY?

I'VE NEVER TASTED BETTER.

THE END.